Redistributive Effects of Canada's Public Pension Programs

SAMUEL A. REA, Jr.

Redistributive Effects of Canada's Public Pension Programs

Available in Canada through

Authorized Bookstore Agents
and other bookstores

or by mail from

Canadian Government Publishing Centre
Supply and Services Canada
Hull, Quebec, Canada K1A 0S9

Catalogue No. EC 22-89/1980E
ISBN 0-660-10696-5

Canada: $4.25
Other Countries: $5.10

Price subject to change without notice

Contents

Tables

Figures

Redistributive Effects of Canada's Public Pension Programs

Redistributive Effects of Canada's Public Pension Programs

The financing of Canada's public pension programs has generated a great deal of controversy. Although the three tiers of public pensions — lump sum Old Age Security pensions (OAS), the contributory Canada Pension Plan and its equivalent, the Quebec Pension Plan (CPP/QPP), and the income-tested Guaranteed Income Supplement (GIS) — promise significant retirement benefits to today's working population, contributions by today's workers (or taxes in the case of OAS and GIS) are not sufficient to finance future benefits.

As a consequence, the partial financing of the programs produces significant redistribution between generations because future workers will have to be taxed in order to provide the benefits that are currently promised. The pattern of this redistribution is affected by future trends in mortality rates, fertility rates, immigration, participation rates, and rates of growth of real earnings.

A second consequence of the underfunding of old age programs is a possible reduction in saving. From a contributor's point of view, public pensions create wealth when the benefits that are promised exceed the contributions in present value. Generations that receive benefits in excess of contributions may be influenced by this "social security wealth" (Feldstein, 1974). The controversial effect of this wealth on saving is not discussed in this paper, but estimates of the magnitude of wealth are provided. These estimates can be used by other researchers who wish to explore saving behaviour.

Complex programs such as the Canada or Quebec Pension Plans are likely to redistribute income, or more precisely wealth, between contributors. The patterns of redistribution are not widely understood because one must know the future life history of a contributor in order to calculate his contributions and benefits. A computer model (Lifesim) capable of simulating individual life histories and calculating pension benefits was developed as part of a study by Pesando and Rea (1977) and improved for this study. Although crude in many ways, the system enables one to explore the redistribution between income classes, cohorts, and individuals of different sex or marital status. These detailed estimates are particularly important at the present time in view of the controversy surrounding provisions of the CPP that would increase benefits for mothers whose earnings fall while their children are young. These provisions have been passed by Parliament but not accepted by Ontario and British Columbia.

The Lifesim model provides estimates of the taxes and contribution rates that will be required to finance future CPP/QPP, OAS, and GIS pension benefits. These figures illustrate the effect of the demographic composition of the population on future tax rates. The simulations also highlight the consequences of a move to a contribution rate for the Canada and Quebec pension plans that would "fully fund" benefits for new entrants. Actuaries refer to this rate as the "entry-age-normal" contribution rate.

THE LIFE SIMULATION SYSTEM

One cannot generalize about the redistributive effects of the Canada Pension Plan without simplifying assumptions. All of the possible variations in life histories must be analysed in order to calculate supplementary benefits and the implications of the plan for different cohorts. Since the CPP/QPP is relatively new, estimates of lifetime payments must be based on a simulation of the future life histories of the current population. Lifesim, a computer simulation system which was developed for this task, generates future life histories for a representative sample of individuals and calculates pension contributions and benefits. The simulation model is explained in detail in the Appendix.

The model collects life histories for a sample of individuals that have the same age, sex, and provincial distribution in 1966 as the actual census distribution. The 1972 Survey of Consumer Finances provides much of the information on labour force participation, earnings, income, unemployment, and duration of unemployment. As each individual ages, he faces probabilities of being in the labour force, being unemployed, and so on. In the simulation system, an individual's annual labour force participation, for instance, is randomly assigned on the basis of estimated probabilities. The result is a complete life history for as many individuals as desired. Most of the simulations reported in this study are based on a 1 in 2,500 sample which was taken from the 1966 population census. The sample consists of approximately 8,000 individuals chosen in 1966 to which new individuals were added in subsequent years as birth and immigration augmented the population. A larger sample (1 in 1,667) is used for some of the simulations, especially those with "medium" demographic growth assumption. In practice, there is relatively little sampling variation between runs for aggregate variables.

For the purposes of analysing the distributional effects of the CPP/QPP, the year to year fluctuations in an individual's earnings are particularly important. The distribution of lifetime earnings and pension credits is affected by these fluctuations. For example, a transitory reduction in earnings to below the basic exemption level may disqualify a contributor from CPP/QPP disability benefits. Unfortunately, there is little information on year to year movement in income, labour force participation, wages, and so on at the microeconomic level. Because of this lack of information, a number of assumptions have to be made in the model. These assumptions are described in the Appendix. Year to year changes in earnings occur in the model in response to variables such as labour force participation, unemployment, self-employment status, education, age, or marital status. In addition, a constant real rate of growth is assumed for earnings and other income.

The difficulty of predicting realistic life histories also turned up in the Orcutt's DYNASIM model, the most elaborate micro simulation model of this type (Orcutt et al, 1976). A comparison of generated life histories with actual life histories revealed that the DYNASIM model included too few women with a long-term commitment to the labour force (Hendricks and Holden, 1976; Holden, 1977).

Similar problems probably occur in the Lifesim model, but there are no longitudinal Canadian data with which to make comparisons. Another drawback to the model is that the cross-section income data on the retired population in 1971 may underestimate the private pension credits being accumulated by today's workers. For this reason, the Lifesim model is not used to draw conclusions concerning the distribution of income among the future retired population. For such purposes, private pension information must be added to the model. A related problem is that future exogenous changes in labour force participation are not included in the model.

The key assumptions concerning fertility, mortality and immigration were provided by Denton et al (1980). In that study, four alternative demographic scenarios were simulated (see Table 1). For purposes of simulation, the 1971 mortality rates were assumed to hold between 1966 and 1990, with changes taking place in 1991 and 2011.[1] The 1971 fertility rates were assumed to hold until 1983 with alternative rates assumed thereafter. Fertility rates influence labour force participation in the model, but no exogenous trends in participation were incorporated.

Table 1

Alternative Demographic Growth Assumptions

	Low	Low-Med	Medium	High
Total fertility rate—1984 onward (children born per woman during her lifetime)	1.5	1.5	2.1	3.0
Yearly immigration—1981 onward (number of individuals)	60,000	120,000	120,000	180,000
Life expectancy at birth—2011 onward (years)				
Male	73.0	71.9	71.9	70.7
Female	85.3	82.3	82.3	79.3

SOURCE Denton et al (1980).

The Lifesim model is modified somewhat from the version reported in Pesando and Rea (1977). The most important changes allow aggregate time series to be calculated for the future. Some changes are made to lower the costs of operating the model, such as use of a more efficient random number generating technique. Finally, modifications are made to the fertility, mortality, and age-sex distribution of immigrants and emigrants.

Given life histories, the second phase of the simulation program calculates the CPP/QPP contributions and benefits for each person. The supplementary benefits such as disability benefits, orphan's benefits, and spouse's benefits are included. Every

Table 2

Simulations

	Simulation number	Deviation from 1978 law	Real earnings growth rate	Real discount rate
			(Per cent)	
Low-medium demographic growth assumptions	L1R1	No change	2.5	2.5
	L1R2	Drop out low years for mothers	2.5	2.5
	L1R3	Pay-as-you-go 2006 onward	2.5	2.5
	L1R4	No division following divorce	2.5	2.5
	L1R5	9.1 per cent contribution rate 1978 onward	2.5	2.5
	L1R6	No change	1.5	2.5
	L1R7	No change	2.5	4.0
Low demographic growth assumptions	L2R1	No change	2.5	2.5
	L2R2	Pay-as-you-go 2004 onward	2.5	2.5
High demographic growth assumptions	L3R1	No change	2.5	2.5
Medium demographic growth assumptions	L4R1	No change	2.5	2.5
	L4R3	Pay-as-you-go 2008 onward	2.5	2.5
	L4R4	Pay-as-you-go 2008 onward	2.5	3.0
	L4R7	Pay-as-you-go 2008 onward, OAS/GIS increase 2.5 per cent per year in real terms	2.5	2.5
	L4R8	9.4 per cent contribution rate, 1978 onward	2.5	2.5
	L4R9	Pay-as-you-go 2008 onward	2.5	5.0

aspect of the plan from 1966 onward is built into the simulation program. One feature of the early years of the plan is ignored: from 1966 onward, it is assumed that spouse's benefits applied to men and women equally, as is now the case. Differences between the QPP and CPP are not taken into account. Income taxes are calculated under the assumption that the income tax system is wage-indexed.

Since the CPP/QPP contributions and benefits are distributed over a lifetime, the present value of net benefits (present value of benefits minus present value of contributions) is calculated in the first year in which the contributor could potentially make contributions. This is either 1966, the year in which he turns 18, or the year in which he enters Canada, whichever is later.[2] The present value calculation requires that one know a real rate of discount as well as a real rate of growth of earnings per worker and the rate of the inflation. It is assumed for most of the simulations that the real rate of growth of earnings per worker is 2.5 per cent, the real rate of discount is 2.5 per cent, and the rate of inflation is 6.0 per cent. These figures are in line with recent experience. The average real rate of growth in wages, salaries and supplements per worker was 2.8 per cent between 1955 and 1974. The rate of return on long-term government bonds averaged 2.2 percentage points above inflation during the same period. The rate of inflation averaged approximately 6.0 per cent between 1966 and 1977; the rate of inflation, however, has only a slight effect on the real present value of the CPP/QPP.[3] Some alternative assumptions are also tested, but no effort is made to model the interrelationship between the rate of growth of earnings, the rate of discount, and variables such as immigration and fertility. The simulations are listed in Table 2.

CANADA'S PENSION LIABILITIES

The present value of the benefits promised by the three public pension programs equals the country's gross social security wealth. If we subtract the present value of contributions, and take account of the tax deductibility of contributions and the taxability of benefits, the result is the country's net social security wealth. This wealth is also called the unfunded liability of the pension system. The unfunded liability is important for two reasons: first, it indicates that there is substantial redistribution between generations implicit in the programs; and, second, it may induce contributors to reduce their private saving for retirement.

Table 3 presents the pension wealth calculated using the "medium" demographic growth assumptions. In 1977, the unfunded liability of the Canada and Quebec pension plans at current contribution rates was $173 billion, nearly equal to gross national product (GNP). The present value of OAS and GIS benefits was $187 billion. If we assume that the tax base for OAS/GIS grows at the same rate as personal income and we deduct the present value of OAS/GIS taxes that must be paid in the future, the net OAS/GIS wealth is $65 billion. The sum of the three programs, the CPP/QPP, OAS and GIS produces net social security wealth equal to $238 billion. As a point of comparison, this sum exceeds 1977 GNP by about 15 per cent. The total value of all plant and equipment in Canada in 1977 equalled $405 billion.[4] However, the social security wealth has been calculated using a relatively low rate of discount compared with the rate of return on fixed capital. A 4 per cent rate of discount lowers the net CPP/QPP wealth by 43 per cent.

Table 3

Social Security Wealth, Canada, 1977

		Billions of 1977 dollars
1	Gross CPP/QPP benefits	262
2	CPP/QPP benefits net of income taxes	210
3	CPP/QPP benefits net of income taxes and contributions	173
4	CPP/QPP benefits net of income taxes and contributions (pay-as-you-go after 2007)	170
5	CPP/QPP benefits net of income taxes and contributions, 9.4 per cent contribution rate after 1977	115
6	OAS benefits net of income taxes	165
7	GIS	22
8	OAS and GIS net of income taxes on benefits and taxes for financing program	65
9	OAS and GIS net of taxes on benefits and taxes for financing program (benefits increase at 2.5 per cent per year in real terms after 1977)	244
10	Total 3 + 8	238
11	Total 4 + 8	235
12	Total 4 + 9	414

Assumes current contribution rates unless otherwise noted.

The net wealth is not altered significantly by including the increases in CPP/QPP contribution rates that will have to be made in order to cover benefits on a pay-as-you-go basis. Under the assumptions of this simulation (run L4R1), the fund will be exhausted in the year 2007. The present value of additional contributions after that year lowers the unfunded liability by only $3 billion (line 4 of Table 3). If contribution rates were increased from 3.6 per cent to 9.4 per cent in 1978, the present value of contributions would equal the present value of benefits for those just entering the labour force. However, the unfunded liability of the CPP/QPP would still be $115 billion (line 5) because of the insufficient contributions during the early years of the programs.

The importance of the enormous social security wealth depends on whether consumers alter their saving behaviour because of the perceived wealth. In fact, the choice between the alternative measures of wealth depends on what is perceived by consumers. If consumers anticipate, for instance, that OAS and GIS benefits will increase along with per capita earnings and contribution rates will remain unchanged, the wealth is even larger (line 3 plus line 9 in Table 3). The saving issue is not examined in this paper, but the wealth estimates provided here should be useful for those estimating the saving response. Table 4 provides a times series for social security wealth under the assumption that the CPP and QPP will be funded on a pay-as-you-go basis after 2007.

THE FUTURE OF THE CPP/QPP: THE IMPACT OF DEMOGRAPHIC ASSUMPTIONS

The CPP/QPP funds are predicted to be exhausted in the year 2007 if contributions are not increased. Thereafter, the contribution rate will have to be increased in order to meet the current benefits. The rate that will finance benefits on a current basis is known as the pay-as-you-go rate. The pay-as-you-go rate is particularly sensitive to changes in demographic assumptions. In general, the pay-as-you-go rate depends on the number of retirees relative to the number of workers because the tax base depends on aggregate earnings. The ratio of pensioners to workers will decrease if the population increases rapidly because of birth or immigration. This occurs despite the reduction in female labour force participation that accompanies an increase in fertility. A decrease in mortality rates will raise the ratio.

Table 4

Social Security Wealth, Canada, 1966-82[1]

Year	Gross CPP/QPP benefits	CPP/QPP benefits net of income taxes	CPP/QPP benefits less contributions net of taxes[2]	OAS net of income taxes	GIS	OAS and GIS net of taxes for financing[3]	Total benefits net of taxes, contributions, and financing
			(Billions of 1977 dollars)				
1966	122	101	82	113	21	68	150
1967	133	109	89	119	22	70	159
1968	143	117	96	124	22	71	167
1969	154	126	103	129	23	71	174
1970	166	135	111	133	23	71	182
1971	177	144	118	138	23	71	189
1972	190	154	126	142	23	71	197
1973	204	165	135	147	23	71	206
1974	219	177	144	152	23	70	214
1975	233	187	152	157	23	68	220
1976	248	199	161	161	23	66	227
1977	262	210	170	165	22	65	235
1978	278	222	179	169	22	62	241
1979	293	234	188	173	21	61	249
1980	308	245	197	177	21	59	256
1981	324	258	206	180	20	58	264
1982	340	270	215	184	19	56	271

1 Run L4R3. The figures represent the present value of benefits for everyone age 18 and over.
2 Pay-as-you-go after 2007.
3 The present value of taxes for OAS and GIS is calculated under the assumption that personal income taxes are used to finance OAS and GIS on a pay-as-you-go basis.

Table 5

CPP/QPP Fund, Pay-As-You-Go Contribution Rate, and OAS Recipients, under Selected Demographic Growth Assumptions, 1990-2050

	CPP/QPP fund									
	3.6 contribution rate			Pay-as-you-go contribution rate				OAS recipients		
	Low	Medium	High	Low	Low-Medium	Medium	High	Low	Medium	High
	(Billions of 1977 dollars)			(Per cent)				(Thousands of people)		
1990	23.0	23.4	23.6	4.3	4.2	4.0	4.3	2,776	2,890	2,893
1995	18.5	19.9	20.2	5.0	4.7	4.6	4.8	3,316	3,300	3,247
2000	9.2	13.5	13.4	5.3	4.7	4.8	4.7	3,635	3,587	3,388
2005	—	2.8	3.5	5.4	5.1	4.9	4.7	3,896	3,789	3,609
2010	—	—	—	6.0	5.6	5.4	4.8	4,244	4,125	3,989
2015	—	—	—	7.2	6.4	6.2	5.0	5,008	4,864	4,517
2020	—	—	—	8.4	7.4	6.7	5.3	5,701	5,480	5,194
2025	—	—	—	9.4	8.4	7.3	5.4	6,419	6,198	5,946
2030	—	—	—	10.0	8.6	7.3	5.3	6,922	6,673	6,503
2040	—	—	—	—	—	7.2	—	—	7,103	—
2050	—	—	—	—	—	7.2	—	—	8,109	—

See Table 1 for a description of the demographic growth assumptions.

Other assumptions: inflation rate 6 per cent, discount rate 8.5 per cent, real rate of growth of earnings, 2.5 per cent.

Table 5 indicates the effect of the demographic assumptions on the CPP/QPP pay-as-you-go rate. Under the medium demographic growth assumption, the pay-as-you-go rate rises to 4.9 per cent by 2005 and to 7.3 per cent by the year 2030. The pay-as-you-go rate in 2030 is roughly what would prevail in subsequent years. If Canada experiences low fertility, low immigration, and low mortality, the pay-as-you-go rate will rise to 10 per cent in 2030. On the other hand, high fertility, high immigration and high mortality produce a rate equal to 5.3 per cent in 2030.

The differences in tax rates are great despite the relatively small differences in the pensioner population (see the last three columns of Table 5). The most significant differences occur in the rates of growth of earnings (Table 6). The low assumption results in an earnings growth in the last decade that is less than the long-term productivity growth (2.0 per cent compared with 2.5 per cent). The high assumption produces nearly constant rates of growth of aggregate earnings from 1977 onward.

Table 6

Annual Rates of Growth of Real Aggregate Earnings, 1977-2030

	Demographic growth assumptions			
Time period	Low	Low-medium	Medium	High
	(Per cent)			
1977-2000	3.96	4.17	4.15	4.46
2000-2010	2.94	3.51	3.68	4.69
2010-2020	2.23	2.56	3.23	4.37
2020-2030	2.06	2.84	3.24	4.47
1977-2030	3.08	3.49	3.72	4.49

Real earnings per worker are assumed to grow at a rate of 2.5 per cent per year.

The choice between pay-as-you-go and full funding of the CPP/QPP is subject to a great deal of current debate. A controversial economic argument suggests that future generations will prefer full funding if the rate of return on capital exceeds the rate of growth of aggregate earnings. The appropriate rate of return on capital is the social rate of return for a closed economy and the private rate of return for an economy with perfect international mobility of capital. The appropriate return is somewhere between these two extremes if the interest elasticity of foreign investment is positive but not infinite. In any case, the private rate of return on capital is almost certainly in excess of 4.4 per cent, the earnings growth rate under the most optimistic assumptions.[5] This relationship suggests that full funding is the appropriate method of financing the CPP/QPP under the criterion mentioned above.[6] An obvious difficulty with the criterion is that full funding will lower the net benefits of current workers.

Although the interrelationship between the funding decision and the capital stock will not be discussed here, the contribution rate generated by the simulations can be used to highlight the logic behind the funding criterion. If the fully funded rate is below the ultimate pay-as-you-go rate, the fully funded method would appear to be preferred by future generations. Under these conditions, future generations are able to pay a lower contribution rate for the same benefit level by purchasing the capital accumulated by the retired population rather than by supporting the retired population through a pay-as-you-go scheme.

The relationship between the pay-as-you-go rate, the fully funded rate, and the funding criterion is illustrated in Table 7. For purposes of this comparison, the "fully funded" rate is the rate that would equate the present value of contributions to the present value of benefits for someone just entering the labour force at age 18. Actuaries call this the entry-age-normal rate. This rate is not sufficient to finance the benefits paid to earlier generations who contributed at a lower rate or for fewer years. In the first column, the pay-as-you-go rate falls below the fully funded rate because the rate of growth of aggregate earnings (2.84 per cent) exceeds the real rate of discount (2.5 per cent). In the second column, a higher rate of discount has no effect on

Table 7

CPP/QPP Contribution Rates, under Selected Rates of Discount and Rates of Growth of Earnings (Low-Medium Demographic Growth Assumptions)

	Simulation number		
	L1R1	L1R7	L1R6
	(Per cent)		
Rate of growth of real earnings	2.5	2.5	1.5
Real discount rate	2.5	4.0	2.5
Pay-as-you-go contribution rate, 2030	8.6	8.6	9.6
Fully funded contribution rate[1]	9.1	5.7	7.5
Annual rate of growth of aggregate earnings, 2020-30	2.84	2.84	1.84

1 Entry-age-normal rate for 1960-64 cohort.

the pay-as-you-go rate but reduces the fully funded rate to 5.7 per cent. These figures illustrate that future generations will prefer the fully funded plan under this set of assumptions. The same conclusion is reached if we compare the rate of discount (4.0 per cent) with the rate of growth of aggregate earnings (2.84 per cent). In the last column, the per capita real earnings growth rate is reduced to 1.5 per cent. This raises the pay-as-you-go contribution rate to 9.6 per cent and lowers the fully funded rate to 7.5 per cent. Again, the real rate of discount (2.5 per cent) exceeds the rate of growth of aggregate earnings (1.84 per cent). The distributional implications of the funding decision for today's population are discussed in subsequent sections.

Some observers have predicted that the total package of public pension benefits would virtually destroy the Canadian economy because of the large pay-as-you-go rates that will be required in the future. Given today's benefit structure and our best estimates of future demographic trends, this concern over future tax rates is unjustified. In Table 8, the ratio of benefits to aggregate earnings is forecast. Because the OAS and GIS are not increased in real terms in line with increases in real per capita income, the benefits actually fall as a percentage of aggregate earnings through the year 2010. The subsequent increase is temporary and relatively modest. However, if Canada experiences low fertility, low mortality, and low immigration, the total share of earnings rises from 4.49 per cent in 1980 to 6.49 per cent in 2030. This is hardly a catastrophic increase.

Two considerations could alter the picture presented in Table 8. First, it is likely that the OAS and GIS will be increased along with average income. This escalation of benefits will raise the share of OAS, for instance, under the medium assumption from 1.39 to 5.14, raising the total benefit share of earnings to 8.61 by 2030. Alternatively, a lower rate of growth of earnings per capita would dampen the relative decline of the OAS and GIS. Under the low-medium assumption, a decrease in the rate of real growth of per capita earnings from 2.5 per cent to 1.5 per cent raises the share of all benefits from 5.6 per cent to 7.4 per cent in 2030. Adjustment of the OAS and GIS for real growth would raise this to at least 11 per cent. One can conclude that a doubling of the ratio of aggregate benefits to aggregate earnings by 2030 is a realistic possibility.

ISSUES IN THE ANALYSIS OF REDISTRIBUTION

Public pension programs have important distribution implications. Some groups may be made substantially better off as a result of the program, but it is difficult to measure this impact. A number of methodological issues arise in the analysis of the lifetime redistribution of income. This study follows the methodology outlined in Pesando and Rea (1977). The key features of this approach are:

1 Redistribution is measured with the changes in wealth that result from a program. The increase in wealth is the present value of future benefits minus

Table 8

Benefits of Various Public Pension Programs as a Percentage of Aggregate Earnings, 1980-2050

	Demographic growth assumption									
	Medium (L4R1)					Low (L2R1)				
Year	OAS	GIS	OAS and GIS	CPP/QPP	Total	OAS	GIS	OAS and GIS	CPP/QPP	Total
	(Per cent)									
1980	2.71	.84	3.55	1.04	4.59	2.56	.81	3.37	1.12	4.49
1990	2.28	.41	2.69	1.87	4.56	2.17	.33	2.50	1.98	4.48
2000	1.91	.18	2.09	2.22	4.31	1.98	.17	2.15	2.40	4.55
2010	1.56	.08	1.64	2.50	4.14	1.76	.07	1.83	2.77	4.60
2020	1.54	.04	1.58	3.14	4.72	1.92	.04	1.96	4.14	6.10
2030	1.39	.02	1.41	3.45	4.86	1.92	.03	1.95	4.54	6.49
2040	1.11	.01	1.12	3.44	4.56	—	—	—	—	—
2050	.91	.01	.92	3.45	4.37	—	—	—	—	—

the present value of future contributions. The net wealth is evaluated in the year in which the individual turns 18. An alternative approach might be to make comparisons with the internal rate of return, the discount rate that would make the present value (or net wealth) equal zero. This approach is not meaningful if the internal rate of return exceeds the market rate of interest because the internal rate of return does not indicate the increase in lifetime consumption that is made possible by the pension program. In many situations, individuals may have very high rates of return on contributions to a public pension program but receive little benefit from the program in absolute terms.

2 In this study, a pension program is arbitrarily defined to be regressive if the amount of wealth transferred rises with lifetime income. Alternatively, one could define a program to be regressive if it increases the inequality of wealth. The definition chosen focuses on the division of the wealth "created" rather than the overall division of wealth. A program is arbitrarily defined to be distributionally neutral if the new wealth is equally distributed.

3 An individual's contributions are assumed to include the contributions that the employer makes on his behalf. This assumption follows from economic research that suggests that, in the long run, wages are decreased by the amount of payroll taxes (Brittain, 1972).

4 The benefits for the CPP/QPP are calculated net of income taxes. This assumption implies that income tax rates are not raised to offset the current loss from the deductibility of contributions. This may not be the case but, in order to observe the relative advantages of tax postponement across income classes, it is necessary to consider the tax deductibility of CPP/QPP contributions and the taxability of benefits.

5 The CPP/QPP benefits are calculated without taking into account reductions in GIS benefits. This approach is reasonable because GIS benefits were designed as a supplement to the CPP/QPP. However, from an individual's point of view, the reduction in GIS benefits resulting from an increase in CPP/QPP benefits lowers the net increase in retirement income provided by CPP/QPP contributions.

6 It is desirable to consider the benefits and contributions as a package, that is, to analyse the net wealth transferred as a result of the program. In the case of OAS and GIS this approach poses two problems. First, these programs are financed out of general revenues. We know relatively little about the incidence of the tax system as a whole. Second, it must be assumed that without OAS and GIS, taxes would be lower. That is, the funds would not be distributed in some other manner. For purposes of analysing intergenerational transfers, it was assumed that OAS and GIS are financed from the personal income tax and that taxes would be lower without the two programs. The incidence assumptions will not affect the intergenerational results.

INTERGENERATIONAL TRANSFERS

Large inter-cohort transfers are caused by the introduction of a pay-as-you-go pension. The introduction of the CPP/QPP in 1966 transferred substantial net wealth to those who received the benefits after making contributions for only a fraction of their working lives. In Table 9, the average benefit in each cohort is presented. For this table and subsequent tables, immigrants entering Canada after age 18 are excluded. The first column under each demographic assumption heading is the average present value of benefits for an individual under the actual law, with no provision for increased contribution rates in the future. Under this scenario, the benefits are financed out of general revenue after the fund is exhausted. The 1925-29 cohort, a group that turns 65 in 1990-94, receives the largest net benefit. This result apparently occurs because the Year's Maximum Pensionable Earnings (YMPE) is scheduled to grow at a 12.5 per cent annual rate until it catches up to average earnings. This should occur in the late 1980s if present trends continue. The ratio of after-tax benefits to after-tax contributions (not shown) is highest for the 1910-14 cohort. The CPP/QPP benefits for this group are 90.4 per cent subsidized by younger workers.[7]

If contribution rates are increased to finance the plan on a pay-as-you-go basis, the net benefits for all those not retired by 2008 are reduced. Table 9 indicates that the net benefits for the 1960-64 cohort fall by 15 per cent when future increases in the contribution rate are taken into account (medium assumption).

Net benefits for the current population rise if future mortality rates fall. Compared with the medium assumption, the 1960-64 cohort receives 16 per cent higher net benefits under the low mortality assumption and 15 per cent lower net benefits under the high mortality assumption. If future contribution rates are adjusted to the pay-as-you-go level, the net benefits of the 1960-64 cohort under the low assumption are still higher than the benefits under the medium assumption. In other words, the greater longevity dominates the difference in the pay-as-you-go rate for this cohort. Future changes

Table 9

Net Lifetime Benefits from CPP/QPP, by Age Cohort, under Various Demographic Growth and Contribution Rate Assumptions

	Contribution rate								
	Low demographic growth		Low-medium demographic growth			Medium demographic growth			High demographic growth
Cohort (year of birth)	3.6 per cent (L2R1)	3.6 per cent—pay/go 2004 onward (L2R2)	3.6 per cent (L1R1)	3.6 per cent—pay/go 2006 onward (L1R3)	9.1 per cent 1978 onward (L1R5)	3.6 per cent (L4R1)	3.6 per cent—pay/go 2008 onward (L4R3)	9.4 per cent 1978 onward (L4R8)	3.6 per cent (L3R1)
	(Thousands of 1977 dollars)								
1895-99	0.12	0.12	0.19	0.19	0.19	0.16	0.16	0.16	0.19
1900-04	0.97	0.97	0.80	0.80	0.80	0.95	0.95	1.09	0.79
1905-09	2.63	2.63	3.21	3.21	3.21	2.82	2.82	3.08	2.70
1910-14	5.98	5.98	5.13	5.13	5.12	5.57	5.57	5.99	6.09
1915-19	7.14	7.14	7.49	7.49	7.22	8.12	8.12	8.16	6.91
1920-24	8.88	8.88	8.33	8.33	7.56	9.03	9.03	8.83	8.82
1925-29	9.97	9.97	10.30	10.30	9.04	9.30	9.30	8.00	9.85
1930-34	9.82	9.82	8.76	8.76	7.04	8.95	8.95	7.27	8.56
1935-39	9.64	9.64	9.66	9.66	7.12	8.54	8.54	5.95	8.16
1940-44	7.91	7.84	7.90	7.87	4.80	8.05	8.05	4.88	7.34
1945-49	8.27	8.00	7.45	7.30	3.65	7.56	7.47	3.65	6.84
1950-54	8.82	8.14	8.63	8.17	3.37	8.34	8.00	2.82	7.71
1955-59	8.81	7.49	8.88	7.95	2.34	8.28	7.53	1.34	7.59
1960-64	10.20	7.93	8.77	6.94	0.62	8.78	7.45	0.73	7.43

Net benefits are present values for an individual in 1966 or the year in which he/she attains age 18, whichever is later, of benefits less taxes on those benefits, minus the present value of contributions. The calculations assume that employees bear the entire burden of contributions.

in demographic assumptions have little impact on older members of today's population. Some of the differences appearing in Table 9 result from sampling error.

If the CPP/QPP becomes fully funded for the 1960-64 cohort, the contribution rate would have to be raised to 9.4 per cent in 1978 under the medium assumption in order to meet future benefit obligations and administrative costs (assumed to equal 4.0 per cent of benefits). This entry-age-normal rate would not finance all future benefits because earlier cohorts would receive benefits in excess of accumulated contributions. Moreover, the after-tax benefits for the 1960-64 cohort would still be positive because of the difference between the marginal tax rate before and after retirement and the advantage of postponing taxes. The average net benefits with a contribution rate of 9.4 per cent after 1977 are presented in column 8 of Table 9. The benefits accruing to the older generation are not significantly affected, but the net benefits to the 1960-64 cohort are near zero. The low demographic growth assumption raises the entry-age-normal rate for the 1960-64 cohort to 10.0 per cent, and the high demographic growth assumption reduces the rate to 8.4 per cent. Mortality rates are largely responsible for these differences.

The OAS and GIS add a considerable amount to each generation's social security wealth. Since these programs are funded with general revenue, it is difficult to apportion the burden of the taxes used to finance the programs. It is assumed that the OAS and GIS programs are funded with personal income taxes on a pay-as-you-go basis. Table 10 presents the present value (in 1966 or at age 18) of OAS and GIS benefits net of the taxes paid to finance the program. Comparisons between generations are misleading because the calculations do not include taxes paid prior to 1966 for the OAS. The table does illustrate that OAS and GIS are the major source of social security wealth for older generations. These same programs actually reduce the wealth of those born after 1940.

Another interesting point is that the total net wealth of the later cohorts is near zero. In fact, if the real discount is 3.0 per cent instead of 2.5 per cent, the total net wealth for the 1960-64 cohort is zero. The wealth of these cohorts would be further reduced if contribution rates were increased prior to the exhaustion of the CPP and QPP funds (see Table 9).

If OAS and GIS were indexed with wages instead of prices, they would increase by 2.5 per cent per year in real terms. The last column of Table 10 shows the net OAS/GIS wealth under these circumstances. In this simulation, the additional OAS benefits are assumed to be untaxed. All cohorts are better off as a result of the change, but the middle cohorts gain the most because they pay increased taxes for OAS and GIS for only a portion of their lives.

Table 10

Net Lifetime Benefits from Public Retirement Income Programs, by Age Cohort and Selected Indexing Assumptions[1]

Cohort (year of birth)	CPP/QPP (L4R3)	OAS/GIS (L4R3)	Total CPP/QPP and OAS/GIS	OAS and GIS wage indexed[2]
		(Thousands of 1977 dollars)		
1895-99	0.16	19.49	19.65	20.49
1900-04	0.95	21.25	22.20	23.58
1905-09	2.82	20.46	23.28	24.24
1910-14	5.57	14.81	20.38	20.55
1915-19	8.12	10.03	18.15	16.70
1920-24	9.03	6.96	15.99	15.25
1925-29	9.30	3.71	13.01	12.79
1930-34	8.95	0.47	9.42	9.87
1935-39	8.54	0.49	9.03	10.96
1940-44	8.05	-2.17	5.88	7.59
1945-49	7.47	-3.75	3.72	4.96
1950-54	8.00	-5.19	2.81	2.45
1955-59	7.53	-5.38	2.15	1.80
1960-64	7.45	-4.76	2.69	2.82

1 Net benefits are present values for an individual in 1966 or the year in which he/she attains age 18, whichever is later. For CPP and QPP the net benefit is the present value of benefits less taxes on those benefits, minus the present value of contributions. For OAS and GIS, the net benefit is the present value of benefits less taxes on those benefits, minus the present value of taxes used to finance the program. It was assumed that OAS and GIS are financed from the personal income tax and that taxes would be lower without the two programs. The calculations assume too that employees bear the entire burden of contributions.

2 OAS and GIS increase each year after 1977 at the same rate as wages, 2.5 per cent in real terms. (Simulation number L4R7). Additional OAS benefits are assumed to be tax-free.

REDISTRIBUTION BETWEEN INCOME CLASSES

The CPP/QPP redistributes income between those in different income or earnings classes. This redistribution is most obvious if we look at net benefits by permanent earnings level.[8] Table 11 illustrates the pattern of benefits for the 1960-64 cohort. At the current contribution rate, the CPP/QPP provides more wealth to those with higher permanent earnings. If contribution rates are increased after 2007 to put the plan on a pay-as-you-go basis, net benefits fall for all groups. An immediate increase in the contribution rate to 9.4 per cent would sharply reverse the pattern. Benefits generally fall with increases in permanent earnings. At the lower level, this is not true because those with very low permanent earnings are likely to be non-contributors for most of their working lives. Those with many years of contributions are able to drop out low earnings years. The dramatic difference between the distributional effects of a fully funded plan and the current plan illustrates that the intergenerational transfers benefit those with higher incomes.

The last column of Table 11 indicates the net wealth when the benefits and contributions are discounted with a 5.0 per cent real rate. Since the net present value is nearly zero for all earnings classes, this is roughly the internal rate of return for the CPP/QPP under the particular set of assumptions chosen.

The distribution of benefits by family income[9] class is more erratic because family income is affected by the spouse's income and to some extent the length of the beneficiary's life. Since income usually falls after retirement, those who live longer tend to have lower permanent incomes. They also receive more retirement benefits. In Table 12, the net benefits are tabulated by broad family income class. The pattern is similar to the earnings pattern but not as pronounced. Those with higher permanent family income receive higher net benefits. If net benefits are divided by permanent family income, net benefits tend to fall as a fraction of permanent income, indicating that the benefits make the distribution of wealth more equitable even if the benefits themselves are not evenly distributed.

When the OAS and GIS benefits are added to the net CPP/QPP benefits, the total benefits are very progressive for the 1910-14 cohort (Table 13). Since the OAS and GIS do not increase in real terms, their

Table 11

Net Lifetime Benefits from CPP/QPP, by Permanent Earnings Class and Contribution Rate, for 1960-64 Cohort

Permanent earnings class	Share of total	Contribution rate: 3.6 per cent (L4R1)	3.6 per cent — pay/go 2008 onward (L4R3)	9.4 per cent 1978 onward (L4R8)	3.6 per cent — pay/go 2008 onward 5 per cent discount rate (L4R9)
	(Per cent)	(Thousands of 1977 dollars)			
0-$500	9	0.09	0.09	0.06	0.01
$500-1,000	10	0.90	0.89	0.74	0.16
$1,000-2,000	10	3.15	3.07	2.28	0.64
$2,000-3,000	5	4.55	4.29	2.61	0.50
$3,000-4,000	5	7.34	6.87	4.15	0.80
$4,000-5,000	3	8.67	8.01	4.37	1.40
$5,000-6,000	3	8.56	7.73	3.15	0.79
$6,000-8,000	6	8.90	7.87	2.42	0.96
$8,000-10,000	4	8.99	7.56	-0.06	0.35
$10,000-12,000	5	10.27	8.75	-0.09	0.00
$12,000-15,000	7	13.55	11.61	0.95	-0.05
$15,000-20,000	9	14.53	11.96	-1.12	-0.70
$20,000-30,000	10	14.18	11.16	-2.85	-0.85
$30,000+	13	15.97	13.22	0.38	0.04
All classes	100	8.78	7.45	0.73	0.14

See note 1 to Table 10.

relative magnitude falls over time. The combined benefits for the 1945-49 cohort are less progressive, and the benefits for the 1960-64 cohort are slightly regressive as defined above.

The total benefit calculations in Table 13 do not include the taxes used to finance the OAS and GIS because their incidence cannot be determined. However, the overall tax system is not likely to be regressive. We can conclude that the total package of old age programs is progressive, but it will become less progressive in the future as the real value of OAS/GIS falls. Ultimately, the group of programs will become more progressive again when pay-as-you-go rates rise to the point where overall net CPP/QPP benefits are zero or negative.

REDISTRIBUTION BASED ON SEX AND FAMILY STATUS

The CPP contains a number of provisions that raise the benefits of contributors with dependents relative to those without dependents. The plan includes survivor's and orphan's benefits, for instance, as well as benefits for children of disabled workers. A more controversial aspect of the program concerns the treatment of housewives. It is often argued that housewives should be compensated for their contribution to household production.

Table 12

Net Lifetime Benefits from CPP/QPP, by Income Class, for 1960-64 Cohort (Medium Demographic Growth Assumptions)

Permanent family income class	Share of total	Net benefits (L4R3)	Net benefits/ permanent family income
	(Per cent)	(Thousands of 1977 dollars)	(Per cent)
0-$5,000	2	0.73	27
$5,000-10,000	8	5.16	66
$10,000-15,000	14	4.97	40
$15,000-20,000	15	8.15	47
$20,000-30,000	24	7.12	29
$30,000+	37	9.21	17
All classes	100	7.45	24

See note to Table 9.

Table 13

Net Lifetime Benefits from Public Retirement Income Programs, by Income Class and Selected Age Cohorts (Medium Demographic Growth Assumptions)

Permanent family income class	1910-14 cohort CPP/ QPP	OAS after tax	GIS	Total	1945-49 cohort CPP/ QPP (L4R3)	OAS after tax	GIS	Total	1960-64 cohort CPP/ QPP (L4R3)	OAS after tax	GIS	Total
							(Thousands of 1977 dollars)					
$500-1,000	0.29	17.54	11.70	29.53	—	—	—	—	—	—	—	—
$1,000-2,000	0.62	16.59	9.51	26.72	—	—	—	—	—	—	—	—
$2,000-3,000	2.85	19.70	6.95	29.50	—	—	—	—	—	—	—	—
$3,000-4,000	4.36	15.46	4.44	24.26	—	—	—	—	—	—	—	—
$4,000-5,000	5.24	14.87	3.55	23.66	—	—	—	—	—	—	—	—
$5,000-6,000	8.03	15.93	3.10	27.06	5.82	5.57	0.56	11.95	—	—	—	—
$6,000-8,000	7.32	13.92	2.35	23.59	4.98	5.28	0.26	10.52	4.36	5.77	0.35	10.48
$8,000-10,000	6.73	12.71	1.48	20.92	5.82	4.65	0.25	10.72	6.00	5.06	0.30	11.36
$10,000-12,000	10.28	11.82	1.23	23.33	7.55	5.01	0.12	12.68	5.68	4.96	0.09	10.73
$12,000-15,000	6.22	10.66	1.06	17.94	7.09	5.58	0.05	12.72	4.53	4.90	0.11	9.54
$15,000-20,000	9.85	10.98	1.01	21.84	7.60	5.79	0.04	13.43	8.15	4.87	0.05	13.07
$20,000-30,000	8.75	8.99	0.78	18.52	8.12	4.62	0.03	12.77	7.12	4.49	0.04	11.65
$30,000 +	6.54	11.34	0.97	18.85	9.45	4.62	0.02	14.09	9.21	4.32	0.01	13.54
All classes	5.57	14.32	3.98	23.77	7.47	5.16	0.16	12.79	7.45	4.58	0.08	12.11

See note 1 to Table 10. For some cohorts the number of individuals in some income classes is too small to be presented.

The current law does compensate housewives (and men in a similar situation) by offering a spouse's allowance in the event that the primary earner dies. In addition, contributions are now divided following a divorce. Parliament has passed another provision that would, in effect, increase benefits for mothers (or single parent fathers) if their earnings are lowered while their children are under seven years of age. This change has not yet gone into effect because it has not received the support of Ontario and British Columbia, but the QPP already includes this provision. The proposed provision and the recently passed divorce rules were simulated in order to determine their cost and distributive effects.

Effective in 1978, a couple's pensionable earnings are to be divided on request following a break-up of a marriage that has lasted at least three years. Contribution credits are divided for each year of marriage (and cohabitation) as long as the couple's average earnings exceed the year's basic exemption and neither person is in receipt of retirement or disability benefits. The provision was simulated with one feature of the law omitted, namely, benefit levels are not recalculated when divorce occurs after benefits become payable.

Few individuals go through their lives without at least one marriage. The effects of the provisions discussed in this section are analysed for those who have had and have not had children. This dichotomy reflects to some extent the duration of marriage and the reduced earnings of women with children.

In Table 14, the average net benefits for a representative cohort is measured. The table includes all members of the cohort. The first column reflects the actual CPP in January 1978. The figures indicate that men with children have higher net benefits than other groups, in part because of spouse's and survivor's benefits which are attributed to their contributions. Women have significantly lower net benefits, particularly if they have had children. For the most part, these differences are due to differences in earnings. As pointed out above, higher net benefits accrue to those with higher earnings. If contributions were raised to the full funding level, the differences would almost disappear. Table 15 indicates the benefits for those with $6,000-8,000 in

Table 14

Net Lifetime Benefits from CPP/QPP, by Family Status and Selected Law, for 1950-59 Cohorts

Family status	Actual law (L1R1)	No division after divorce (L1R4)	Drop-out provisions for mothers (L1R2)
	(Thousands of 1977 dollars)		
Men with no children born	10.84	10.92	10.84
Men with children	13.08	13.22	13.04
Women with no children born	6.70	6.63	6.70
Women with children	4.49	4.35	5.45
Total	8.76	8.77	9.15

See note to Table 9.

Table 15

Net Lifetime Benefits from CPP/QPP, by Selected Family Status and Selected Law, $6,000-8,000 Permanent Earnings Class, 1950-59 Cohorts

Family status	Actual law (L1R1)	Drop-out provisions for mothers (L1R2)	Difference
	(Thousands of 1977 dollars)		
Men with children	11.03	11.01	-0.02
Women with children	11.29	13.97	+2.68

See note to Table 9.

permanent earnings. Women with children receive more benefits than men because of their greater longevity.

A simulation was run in which the division of contributions provision was eliminated from the law. This simulation is captured in column 2 of Table 14. The results indicate that men are better off without the division and women are worse off, particularly those who have had children. The extent of the redistribution is small on average, but much greater for specific cases in which division takes place. The total benefits are increased by only 0.2 per cent. This increase occurs because the division adds to the number of contributors. Some of the benefits have a flat rate component that does not depend on the level of contributions.

The provision that would drop out years of low earnings for mothers (or single parent fathers) is somewhat complicated. When a woman is eligible for any CPP benefit, the benefit calculation is revised to exclude low earnings years when her children are under seven years of age. First, the years in which earnings are below the year's basic exemption are excluded from the benefit calculations. That is, the earnings in these years are not averaged and the length of the contributory period is reduced accordingly. Second, the remaining years' earnings are averaged after adjusting all the years' earnings for changes in the Year's Maximum Pensionable Earnings. Finally, years in which earnings are below the average and children are under seven are excluded from subsequent calculations.[10] The benefits are then calculated as before, with additional drop-out years permitted. The effect of the provisions is to raise benefits for many women who have had children, without increasing their contributions.

The simulation of the drop-out provisions, added to the existing law, produced the average net benefits reported in column 3 of Table 14. The results indicate that the average woman with children receives a 21.5 per cent increase in benefits as a result of the proposed changes. There is a small decrease for men with children because spouse's benefits fall when the spouse's own benefits are increased. The simulation did not include single parent fathers with children under seven years of age.

The increased benefits for mothers tend to help those with higher levels of earnings because the provisions provide a percentage increase in benefits. In other words, those with higher benefits receive a greater absolute increase in benefits. Table 16 illustrates the increase in benefits classified by perma-

Table 16

Net Lifetime Benefits from CPP/QPP, by Permanent Earnings Class and Selected Law, Women with Children, 1950-59 Cohorts

Permanent earnings class	Actual law (L1R1)	Drop-out provisions for mothers (L1R2)	Increase	Increase/ permanent earnings
	(Thousands of 1977 dollars)			
0-$499	0.32	0.43	0.11	0.39
$500-999	1.96	2.47	0.51	0.69
$1,000-1,999	3.59	4.43	0.84	0.57
$2,000-2,999	6.43	7.65	1.22	0.50
$3,000-3,999	5.56	6.73	1.17	0.34
$4,000-4,999	7.98	9.65	1.67	0.37
$5,000-5,999	10.38	12.64	2.26	0.41
$6,000-7,999	11.29	13.97	2.69	0.38
$8,000+	14.51	17.17	2.66	0.18

See note to Table 9.

nent earnings level. The added benefits rise substantially with earnings. The pattern is not so marked when the increase in benefits is compared across family income classes.

The average benefits do not reflect the fact that the drop-out provision will raise the total contribution rate for everyone. The pay-as-you-go rate in 2030 would increase about 0.3 percentage points as a result of the change. The increase in contribution rates would lower the net benefits received by men and women without children.

SUMMARY

A series of microeconomic simulations of Canada's public pension programs leads to the following conclusions.

1 The social security wealth of Canada is very large — $449 billion in 1977 gross of contributions. If contributions and taxes are deducted, the net wealth in 1977 is $235 billion. This wealth could have a substantial effect on private saving.

2 Future immigration, mortality and fertility have a significant effect on the pay-as-you-go rate in the CPP/QPP. Estimates for 2030 range between 5.3 per cent and 10 per cent, with the best estimate equal to 7.3 per cent.

3 The contribution rate that would finance the 1960-64 cohort is 9.4 per cent. This rate, the entry-age-normal rate, varies between 8.4 per cent and 10 per cent, depending on the mortality assumptions. If the real rate of discount is raised to 4.0 per cent, the entry-age-normal rate falls from 9.1 per cent to 5.7 per cent under one demographic scenario.

4 The share of aggregate earnings going to the CPP/QPP, OAS, and GIS will remain relatively constant through 2050 if the plans are not altered and the medium demographic assumptions hold. However, escalation of OAS and GIS in real terms or lower rates of increase in population will increase the share.

5 The 1925-29 cohort receives the highest net benefits from the CPP/QPP. The net benefits of subsequent cohorts fall dramatically if contribution rates are increased in the future.

6 Those currently entering the labour force receive little *net* benefit from the sum of all public programs even if CPP/QPP contribution rates are not increased until the fund is exhausted.

7 The CPP/QPP tends to transfer wealth to higher-income individuals. As contribution rates rise for those not yet born, the program will eventually become progressive.

8 Lower-income individuals receive significantly higher wealth than higher-income individuals from the sum of net CPP/QPP, OAS, and GIS benefits. For those just entering the labour force, this relationship is much less pronounced because the CPP/QPP becomes relatively more important than OAS and GIS benefits. The sum of the three programs will be progressive for future generations that pay much higher contribution rates.

9 Women receive much lower net CPP/QPP benefits than men because of their lower earnings. If earnings are held constant, women receive slightly larger benefits because of their longevity.

10 Division of contributions following divorce has relatively little average distributional impact.

11 The proposed drop-out provisions for mothers raise the benefits for women with children by 22 per cent. The pay-as-you go rate in 2030 is increased by 0.3 percentage points as a result of this change.

Appendix: The Life Simulation System

The Lifesim model generates the life histories of a sample of Canadians using Monte Carlo techniques. The sample population is augmented by those born in the future and those immigrating into Canada. The system allows one to examine income distribution effects of any government transfer program at one point in time or over a lifetime. It also allows one to predict aggregate taxes and benefits and to analyse the implications of changes in specific program parameters. The system consists of two parts: a program to generate the life histories, and a program to apply a particular public program to the individual life histories. These two programs will be discussed in turn.

THE GENERATION OF LIFE HISTORIES

The model is a further development of the Micro Simulation System developed by Dobell and Cohen (1975). A sample of individuals is created given the Canadian population in a base year cross-classified by single years of age, sex, and province. Histories are generated so that the resulting sample will have the same age, sex, and provincial distribution in the base year (1966 for the analysis of the Canada Pension Plan) as the actual census distribution. Figures A-1, A-2, and A-3 summarize the model. Below is a description of how the variables are generated.

1 Marital Status and School Enrolment

Initial characteristics of the population age 18 and over are established through a Monte Carlo process. Marital status, educational achievement, spouse's age, and spouse's educational achievement are randomly assigned based on probability matrices developed by Cohen and Dobell. Individuals are not matched up in families, but the characteristics of the spouse (male or female) are known. From the base year onward, the probabilities of changing marital status, continuing in school, and so on are used to update the individual's record on an annual basis. When a divorce occurs, the woman is assumed to have custody of the children. This part of the system was developed by Cohen and Dobell.

Figure A-1

Life Simulation System: Initial Characteristics

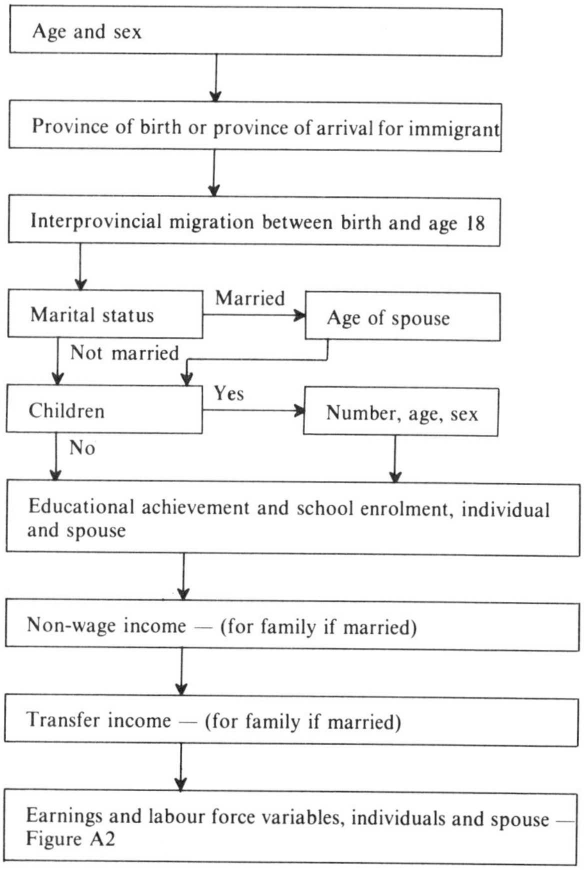

NOTE Characteristics for individuals at age 18, for individuals 18 or over in 1966, or new immigrants over age 18.

Figure A-2

Life Simulation System: Labour Force Variables

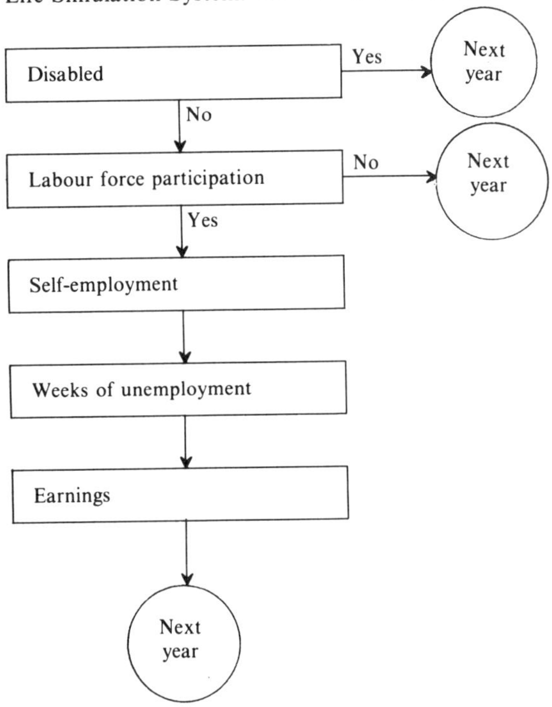

2 Number of Children Present in Base Year

The number of children in a family in the base year (or the number of children in a family that immigrates) was estimated from the 1972 Survey of Consumer Finances. First, the probability of having children aged 0 to 5 (or 6 to 15) was estimated using least squares regression, then the number of children was estimated for those with children. The dependent variables were age and education of husband and wife (if married) and province. A random number determines whether a person has children present in the base year, and the number of children is predicted from the second equation. In order to determine the number of children, an error term for the regression equation is drawn from a normal distribution with mean zero and standard deviation equal to the standard error of estimate for the regression. The procedure was also applied to children aged 6 to 15. The ages of the children are arbitrarily assigned within the under-5 and 6-to-15 intervals. A maximum of 9 children is allowed.

3 Number of Dependent Children

Since orphan benefits and disabled contributors children's benefits under the Canada Pension Plan are payable to children under 18 and single students under 25, the number of such children is updated each year. For those 18 and over, the probability of leaving school was calculated from Statistics Canada school enrolment figures (Canada, 1972, p. 162). Since over 81 per cent of those in university are not married, those in school are assumed to be dependents (Canada, 1974a). The annual school activity status for an individual, as opposed to his children, is predicted from a much more detailed transition matrix (Dobell and Cohen, 1975).

4 Birth

Age-specific fertility rates are applied annually to each female to predict whether children are born. The age-specific fertility rates were obtained from Denton et al (1980).

Those born after the base year enter the system as adults 18 years after birth. The number of births per province is recorded, and after allowing for interprovincial migration before age 18 and child mortality, the 18 year olds are treated just as someone in the base year. In other words, they are assigned initial characteristics such as education and marital status at age 18.

5 Deaths

Age-specific mortality rate projections were provided by Denton et al (1980).

6 Emigration

The age-sex distribution (single years of age) of emigrants has been estimated by Denton et al (1980). The probability of an individual leaving Canada is equal to the proportion of emigrants of his age and sex multiplied by the assumed number of emigrants per year (40,000) and divided by the population in that age and sex category in the base year. This probability is kept constant over time, implying that if the Canadian population increases, an increasing absolute number of individuals will become emigrants. Denton et al (1980) assume that the number of emigrants per year is constant in the future. It is assumed that once an individual emigrates, he does not return. He may, however, collect retirement benefits while abroad.

7 Immigration

The age-sex distribution of immigrants has also been estimated by Denton et al (1980). This to-

Figure A-3

Life Simulation System: Annual Update for Individual

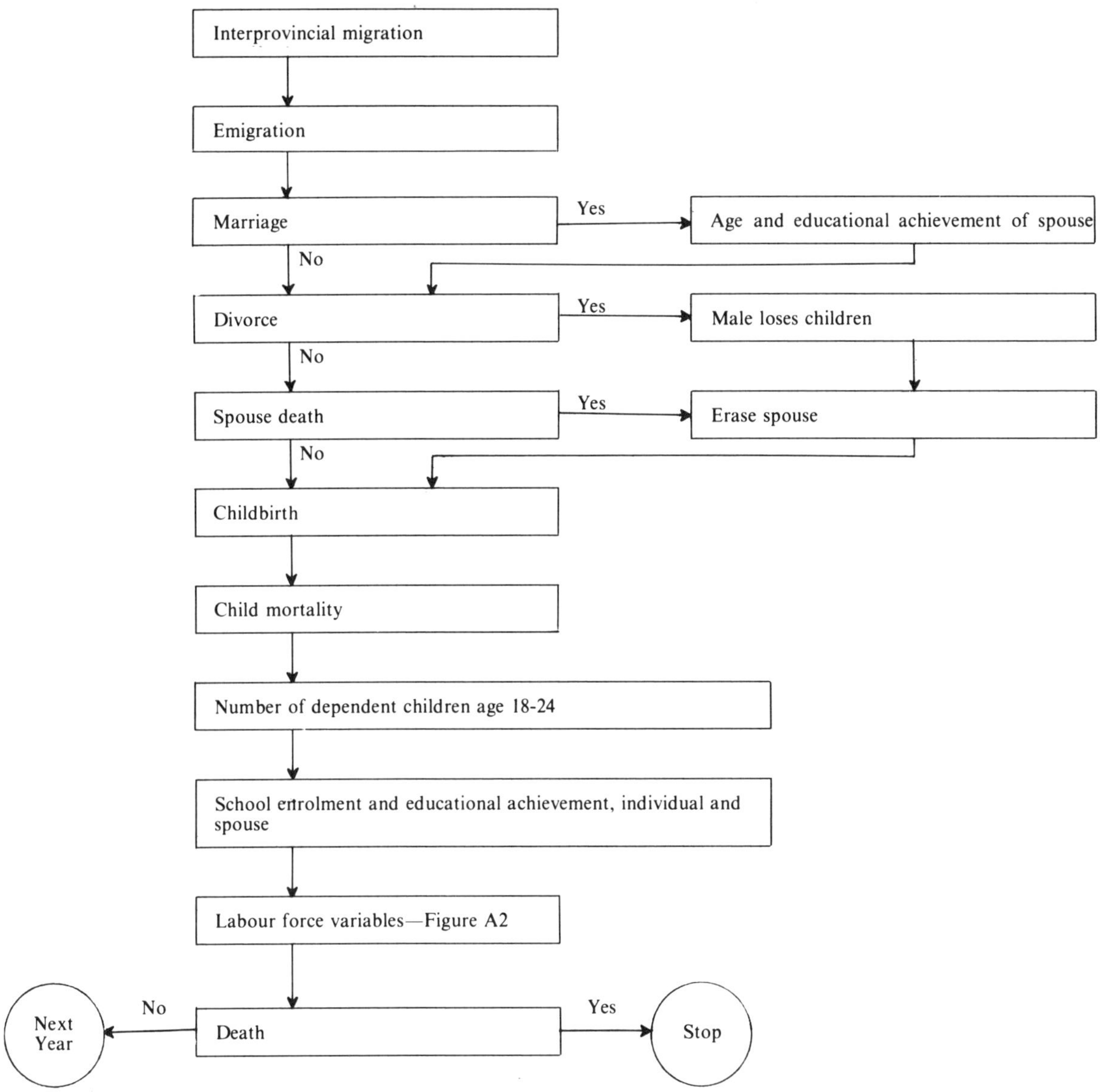

gether with the 1971 to 1973 provincial distribution of immigrants (Canada, 1975) allows one to introduce the immigrants into the system just as those in the base year are introduced. Alternative assumptions were made concerning the number of immigrants entering per year.

8 Interprovincial Migration

Each year, the individuals in the system face the probability of migrating between provinces. The 1971 Census provides information on the age-sex composition of interprovincial migrants and the distribution of province of destination by province of origin in the 1966 to 1971 period (Canada, 1974b). These figures combined with estimates of the annual gross flow during this period (Canada 1974c, p. 50) allow one to calculate the probability of migration by age, sex, and province. For those who are migrants, another probability distribution is used to determine the new province. The age and sex probabilities are assumed independent of the provincial migration propensities. Migration is assumed to equal zero after 1979.

9 Disability

Disability is assigned to individuals in order to calculate their Canada Pension Plan disability benefits. The incidence of disability is taken from the Department of Insurance (Canada, 1973a). It is assumed that, once disabled, one remains disabled for life. This is a reasonable assumption since relatively few of those collecting disability benefits under the CPP go back into the labour force.[11] Disability as well as labour force participation and other variables are assigned to the spouse as well as to the individual whose record is being examined, (the "sample individual").

10 Labour Force Participation

The probability of being in the labour force during the year (defined here as having worked during the year) was estimated from the 1972 Survey of Consumer Finances. Separate regressions were run for married men, married women, single men, and single women.[12] The independent variables are age, sex, education, province, presence of children, and school enrolment. The predicted probabilities are used to assign labour force status. One modification is made to the probabilities. It was assumed when someone over 53 years of age withdraws from the labour force for a year, he stays out of the labour force. In addition, those who are disabled are assumed to be out of the labour force.

11 Self-Employment

The probability of being self-employed (for those who work) was estimated from the Survey of Consumer Finances. The regressions contained age, education, and province. The province coefficients were particularly large because of the geographic concentration of farms. The self-employment variable is created at age 21, and once self-employed, one is assumed to remain self-employed unless he changes provinces, marries before thirty, or leaves school. In these cases, self-employment is reassigned, depending on the estimated probability and a random number. If one is not self-employed at age 21, one could still become self-employed at a later age when a transitional probability of becoming self-employed is compared with a random number.

12 Unemployment

The probability of being unemployed during a year and the duration of unemployment were estimated from the Survey of Consumer Finances. The independent variables were age, education, school enrolment, province, sex, and self-employment. Separate regressions were run for married men, married women, and single men and women. For those with unemployment, the duration equation (weeks of unemployment) was estimated in logarithmic form. Duration was assigned in the simulation by combining the predicted duration with an error obtained from a normal distribution with a standard deviation equal to the standard error of estimate for the regression.

13 Earnings

The logarithm of annual earnings was estimated from the 1972 Survey of Consumer Finances. Separate regressions were run for married men, married women, single men, and single women. The independent variables were province, education, age, presence of children, school enrolment, and duration of unemployment (in step function form). The inclusion of variables which affect labour supply is justified because the number of hours worked affects earnings. The use of the log of earnings implies a log normal distribution of earnings. There is some evidence that the log normal distribution is a good approximation of the earnings distribution,[13] but when the standard error of estimate of the regression equation was applied to a log normal distribution, the resulting errors were too large. In order to more closely replicate the 1971 distributions, earnings were assigned using the predicted values plus an error term with a standard deviation equal to one-half (0.4 for women) the standard error of estimate in the regression equations.

A particularly crucial problem for a lifetime simulation is the correlation of earnings between years. A similar problem exists with labour force participation and unemployment. Unfortunately, there is little information on the year to year movements in an individual's earnings and other income items. One of the few sources of information is a panel study carried out by the survey research centre, University of Michigan (Benus, 1974). A study of five-year income patterns for individual families found a high degree of stability among upper-income groups and found that labour income was the major source of instability (Benus, 1974, pp. 292-93).

The model as described so far allows for instability because of changes in age, education, marital status, children, province, and duration of unemployment. Therefore, the same error term in an individual's earnings equation is applied throughout his life, with a few exceptions. An error term is generated at age 18 and again at the age of marriage if the age of marriage is less than 30. At marriage, earnings of the spouse are generated given his or her characteristics.

14 Income Other Than Earnings

Other income is divided into investment income and transfer income. The latter does not include payments for Old Age Security, the Canada Pension Plan, or the Quebec Pension Plan. The procedure followed was essentially the same as for earnings. The probabilities of having each of the two types of incomes were estimated for married couples and single individuals. The logarithm of the amount of each of these incomes was estimated separately for married couples and single individuals with each of these income types. The two income items are initially predicted at age 18 but new error terms are generated in the year of marriage if under age 30. When over age 30, the new married couples' investment and transfer income are set equal to the sum of the husband's and wife's income as single individuals. The new error term is the difference between this sum and the mean income for married couples with their characteristics. From then on, changes in income occur as predicted by the married couple's income equation. The spouse's income as a single individual must be predicted at the time of marriage. In the case of divorce, the married couple's investment and transfer income is divided and, in the case of the death of the spouse, the individual receives the couple's income.

Investment income was assigned to individuals based on a log normal distribution with the standard error of estimate used as the standard deviation. In the case of transfer income, values in excess of 9,999 were set equal to 9,999.

THE CANADA PENSION PLAN ANALYSER

In the second part of the simulation system, the contributions and benefits under the Canada Pension Plan are calculated for each of the life histories generated by the first part of the simulation system. In each year, the individual's income items are updated by the rate of inflation and rate of growth of real income assumed by the program user. Contributions, including employer contributions, to the Canada Pension Plan (or the Quebec Pension Plan) are calculated for the individual and his spouse. As the contributor qualifies for benefits, whether they be for disability, the death of a spouse, or retirement, the benefits are calculated. For an individual who is still employed after age 65, the program calculates the advisability of claiming benefits before age 70 given the mortality rates and the discount rate.

The calculation of the spouse's contributions and benefits requires some special techniques. At the time of marriage, the age, education, disability, employment, self-employment, unemployment, earnings, and other income are predicted for the spouse. The spouse's past contribution record is not available. In order to remedy this deficiency, whenever a marriage takes place, the ratio of earnings to the Year's Maximum Pensionable Earnings, averaged over the contribution period up to the year of marriage, is stored along with the number of years in the contribution period. This information is kept in a "marriage bank" classified by sex, education, and age of marriage. When a marriage takes place, the prior contribution record of the spouse is picked up from the marriage bank, given the spouse's sex, education, and age of marriage. In effect, the nearest person on the tape with the spouse's characteristics is assumed to be the spouse.

In order to calculate the present value of survivor's benefits, it is necessary to know the future marital status and mortality of the survivors. The program does not follow the spouse after an individual dies. Therefore, information concerning the spouse is picked up from a previous record. When someone dies whose spouse had died previously (and was eligible for survivor's benefits), the present value of the earnings related spouse's benefits divided by the spouse's pension benefits is stored. The present value is calculated at the time the contributor died. Similarly, the present value of the fraction of flat benefits received[14] and the present value of orphan's benefits are stored. When retirement or disability benefits are received in addition to survivor's benefits, both the earnings related benefit and flat benefit are adjusted. This information allows an estimate to be made of the value of survivor's benefits at the time of the contributor's death. The three items are retrieved from the last person on the tape whose sex, education, and age were the same at the time of the spouse's death. The present value of the earnings ratio that is retrieved is multiplied by the deceased contributor's pension calculated at death. The flat spouse benefit for the year of death is multiplied by the present value of the flat benefits received. The sum of these two terms is the present value of the surviving spouse's benefits at the time of the death of the contributor. The present value of orphans' benefits is similarly calculated.

Table A-1

Variables Created

Constant characteristics
SO (1) = sex
1 = male
2 = female
SO (2) = year of arrival in Canada (if immigrant)
SO (3) = province of birth or arrival (1, . . ., 10)
1 = Newfoundland
2 = Prince Edward Island
3 = Nova Scotia
4 = New Brunswick
5 = Quebec
6 = Ontario
7 = Manitoba
8 = Saskatchewan
9 = Alberta
10 = British Columbia
SO (4) = year of birth (cohort identifier)
SO (5) = sex of spouse
1 = male
2 = female
SO (6) = year of leaving Canada (if emigrant)
SO (7) = age at death

Time-dependent characteristics
S (T, 1) = Marital status
0 = single
1 = married
2 = widowed
3 = divorced
S (T, 2) = age of marriage (most recent)
S (T, 3) = no. of children born
S (T, 4) = no. of dependent children
S (T, 5) = educational achievement category
1 = elementary
2 = some secondary
3 = secondary graduate
4 = some post-secondary/non-university
5 = some post-secondary/university
6 = post-secondary grad./non-university
7 = university first degree (BA, BSc)
8 = university second degree (MA, MSc)
9 = university third degree (PhD)
S (T, 6) = no. of years in post-secondary school
S (T, 7) = no. of weeks unemployed in year
99 = out of labour force
S (T, 8) = disabled
1 = disabled
S (T, 9) = self-employed
1 = self-employed
S (T, 10) = earnings
S (T, 11) = age difference of spouse (spouse age – sample individual's age)
S (T, 12) = spouse's educational achievement
S (T, 13) = no. of weeks spouse unemployed in year
99 = out of labour force
S (T, 14) = spouse disabled
1 = disabled
S (T, 15) = spouse self-employed
1 = self-employed
S (T, 16) = spouse's earnings
S (T, 17) = unearned income
S (T, 18) = transfer income
S (T, 19) = total income
K (T) = activity index
1 = grade 9
2 = grade 10
3 = grade 11
4 = grade 12
5 = grade 13
6 = CAAT 1
7 = CATT 2
8 = CAAT 3
9 = univ. 1
10 = univ. 2
11 = univ. 3
12 = univ. 4
13 = univ. 5
14 = univ. 6
15 = univ. 7
16 = univ. 8
17 = univ. 9
18 = univ. 10
20-22 = not in school
KS (T) = spouse activity index
H (T) = province
1 = Nfld
2 = PEI
3 = NS
4 = NB
5 = Quebec
6 = Ont
7 = Man
8 = Sask
9 = Alta
10 = BC

If a contributor dies and leaves orphans and no spouse, the value of orphans' benefits cannot be obtained in the manner described above because the spouse's characteristics are not applicable. Furthermore, the aggregate value of orphans' benefits would be understated if the benefits paid to true orphans (both parents deceased) were not included. Since the age pattern of children is not known, it is necessary to obtain this information from another record. Whenever a contributor dies leaving children but no spouse, the time pattern of orphans' benefits is accessed from the previous family with the same number of children, sex of contributor, and age of contributor. This permits the aggregate benefits to be correctly calculated and the present value of orphans' benefits to be calculated at the time the contributor dies.

The program also calculates the benefits for Quebec residents under the assumption that the Quebec Pension Plan is identical to the Canada Pension Plan. There are some differences between the two plans, but the estimates for Quebec should be approximately correct.

Old Age Security and Guaranteed Income Supplement benefits are calculated. Income taxes are calculated with the 1974 tax laws. It is assumed that the tax system is fully indexed for real growth as well as price changes after 1974. The available income information does not permit the calculation of capital gains and losses, medical expenses, and so on. Exemptions for children, disability, and old age, are included as are deductions for unemployment insurance and CPP contributions. It is assumed that the spouse with the highest earnings (or retirement income) pays taxes on the married couple's investment and transfer income. The tax rates for provinces other than Ontario are arbitrarily set equal to Ontario's. The Ontario Tax credit is calculated under the assumption that 15 per cent of income is spent on housing.[15]

Notes

1 Denton et al (1980) interpolate the mortality rates between these years. This procedure was not practical in the micro-simulation system. The simulation system produced a total population over 65 in 2021 that fell below Denton's forecast by an average of only 2.6 per cent. Part of this difference can be explained by greater emigration in the micro-simulation system. The system holds the probability of emigrating constant rather than the absolute number of emigrants. Population figures for other age groups were not calculated.

2 For purposes of benefit calculation, the contribution period for immigrants includes years since age 18 (or 1966).

3 Inflation affects the rate at which the Years's Maximum Pensionable Earnings catches up to the average wage and also affects real pensions to a small extent because of the three-year time lag in the pension calculation.

4 Canada (1977), p. 1.

5 Jenkins (1977); Feldstein and Summers (1977).

6 Another criterion would be the amount of intergenerational redistribution that is desired.

7 The percentage subsidy is substantially the same for the 1900-19 cohorts.

8 Permanent earnings are calculated by computing the present value at age 18 of earnings up to age 65 (or death). The result is converted into an annuity with constant purchasing power between ages 18 and 65 (or death, if death occurs before age 65).

9 The permanent family income is calculated by computing the present value of lifetime income, including the spouse's income, at age 18 and converting this wealth into a life annuity with constant purchasing power.

10 The number of years remaining must not fall below 10.

11 About two-thirds of the disabled are age 55 and over.

12 Single includes divorced, widowed, and separated.

13 See Blinder (1974) for a review of the literature.

14 Discounting is done using a real rate of discount.

15 15.2 per cent of total expenditure was spent on shelter in 1969, Canada (1973b), p. 66.

Bibliography

BENUS, Jacob. 1974. "Income Instability." In *Five Thousand American Families*, edited by James N. Morgan et al, Ann Arbor: University of Michigan, Survey Research Center, pp. 277-304.

BLINDER, Allan S. 1974. *Toward an Economic Theory of Income Distribution*. Cambridge, Mass.: M.I.T. Press.

BRITTAIN, John A. 1972. *The Payroll Tax for Social Security*. Washington, D.C.: The Brookings Institution.

CALVERT, Geofrey N. 1977. *Pensions and Survival*. Toronto: Financial Press Books.

CANADA. 1972. Statistics Canada. *Estimated Participation Rates in Canadian Education, 1968-69*. Statistics Canada cat. no. 81-552.

____. 1973a. Department of Insurance. *Canada Pension Plan, Statutory Actuarial Report 3*. Ottawa: Supply and Services Canada.

____. 1973b. Statistics Canada. *Family Expenditure in Canada, 1969*. Vol. 1, Statistics Canada cat. no. 62-535.

____. 1974a. Statistics Canada. *1971 Census of Canada*. Vol. 1, Part 5, Statistics Canada cat. no. 92-741-751.

____. 1974b. Statistics Canada. *1971 Census of Canada, Population: Internal Migration*. Vol. 1, Part 2, Statistics Canada cat. no. 92-713-721.

____. 1974c. Statistics Canada. *Population Projections for Canada and the Provinces, 1972-2001*. Statistics Canada cat. no. 91-514.

____. 1975. Department of Manpower and Immigration. *Immigration Statistics*. Ottawa: Supply and Services Canada.

____. 1977. Statistics Canada. *Fixed Capital Flows and Stocks, 1973-77*. Statistics Canada cat. no. 13-211.

DENTON, Frank et al. 1980. *The Future Population and Labour Force of Canada: Projections to the Year 2051*. Economic Council of Canada. Ottawa: Supply and Services Canada.

DOBELL, A. Rodney and COHEN, Morris A. 1975. "Synthetic Longitudinal Sampling and its Application to Public Policy Analysis." Unpublished, mimeo.

FELDSTEIN, Martin and SUMMERS, Lawrence. 1977. "Is the Rate of Profit Falling?" *Brookings Papers on Economic Activity* 1: 211-228.

FELDSTEIN, Martin. 1974. "Social Security Induced Retirement and Aggregate Capital Accumulation." *Journal of Political Economy* 82: 905-26.

GORDON, Nancy M. 1978. "The Treatment of Women in the Public Pension Systems of Five Countries." Urban Institute, Working Paper 5069-01, Washington, D.C.

HENDRICKS, Gary and HOLDEN, Russell. 1976. "A Report on the Variance in Simulated Earnings Histories Produced by DYNASIM." Urban Institute, Working Paper 5075-01, Washington, D.C.

HOLDEN, Russell. 1977. "Components of Variation in Longitudinal Earnings Histories." Urban Institute, Working Paper 5075-02, Washington, D.C.

JENKINS, Glenn. 1977. "Capital in Canada: Its Social and Private Performance 1965-74." Economic Council of Canada Discussion Paper 98, Ottawa.

ORCUTT, Guy et al. 1976. *Policy Exploration Through Micronalytic Simulation*. Urban Institute, Washington, D.C.

PESANDO, James E. and REA, Samuel A., Jr. 1977. *Public and Private Pensions in Canada: An Economic Analysis*. Ontario Economic Council. Toronto: University of Toronto Press.